For many people, the fascination of history is that, as we study, we must continually revise our concepts to incorporate new knowledge which alters our understanding of the period. Each new discovery becomes a revelation. All along, though, we have to accept that without having been there at the time, our insights will always be patchy and incomplete.

Buckfast Abbey is perhaps a place where history becomes easier to comprehend. Imagine a typical day at the monastery...

In the pre-dawn darkness, the monks take their places in the church for Matins - the first of six daily services. A few sleepy guests wake early to join the community in the unchanging order of the Divine Office, before going to the refectory for breakfast.

After Mass, one of the monks and a lay-worker can be seen walking through the woods by the River Dart discussing replanting schemes, while another group of lay-workers erect scaffolding to re-point an area of crumbling stonework on one of the many ancient buildings around the Abbey. Two of the monks make their way to the apiary to tend the bees while, in the office, the Procurator drafts a letter to a local property owner concerning a disputed right of way. The Abbot meets a party of local dignitaries while the Novice Master discusses theology with a group of younger monks.

As the day progresses, traders arrive to stock the Abbey kitchen with locally-produced food for the community, while others take away the monks' own products for sale. Visitors arrive through one of the arched gateways of the Abbey; they have travelled by the main route through the South West peninsula and are stopping at Buckfast for refreshment - both spiritual and physical - before continuing their journey.

At the end of the day, the monks return to the church for Compline, before turning in for an early night, ready for the early start in the morning.

A typical day at Buckfast Abbey in the 20th century? All the events described above could also have taken place at Buckfast on a typical day in the 11th, 14th, or 16th century. What makes Buckfast extraordinary is that it is the only English medieval monastery to have been restored and used again for its original purpose. The monks pray, work and study in the exact spot that their predecessors did nearly a thousand years ago.

THE FIRST ABBEY AT BUCKFAST

For many years the date of the foundation of Buckfast Abbey was a mystery, until one of the monks, searching through a collection of documents in the late 1950s, came upon a reference to the year 1018 as the date of its foundation, in the reign of Cnut. The evidence for this date was scanty, but fairly convincing. No actual foundation charter has survived but after the Dissolution William Petre, who had bought the Abbey's largest manor at South Brent, wanted to ascertain his grazing rights on Dartmoor. His steward made a study of the Abbey's cartulary (collection of charters)[1] and made the following reference in a document of 1557:

ITEM how that Kyng Knout [Cnut] *at instance of Aylward Duk* [i.e.Earl] *first founder of the seid Abbey yn the yer of our lord God mxviii* [1018] *with gode and faithfull words founded the seid Abbey in pure almoyne reservying but only prayer and named the landes yn the same in Danis* [i.e. Anglo-Saxon] *spech and willed by ther writyng of the same that all they that wolde ayde and helpe to the same shud be partakers of the seid prayers - and that all they that did mynysshe and hurt the same to have Christes course* [curse] *and theres as apperith by ii copyes of the seid foundacion yn the seid Register boke* [i.e. the Abbey's cartulary].[2]

The document describes how the foundation of the Abbey was due to Earl 'Aylward', and was confirmed by King Cnut. 'Aylward' was probably the 'Aethelweard' who was made Ealdorman of the western counties in 1016. The Danish King Cnut's invasion and subsequent victory over the Saxons in 1016 was followed - like the Norman invasion fifty years later - by a period of consolidation as the new regime established itself. Cnut recognised that monasteries were stabilising and civilising influences, and founded several during his reign. He also became a close friend of Lyfing, Abbot of Tavistock, who could have had a part in the foundation of Buckfast.

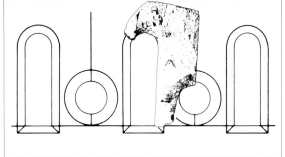

A STONE WINDOW-SLAB WHICH MAY BE THE ONLY EVIDENCE OF THE SAXON MONASTERY.

Before the discovery of this confirmation, historians had all favoured an earlier date for the foundation of Buckfast. A string of other abbeys in the South West were founded from Glastonbury between 960 and 993,[3] and there is good reason to link Buckfast with these. Moreover, more recent research has shown that the great majority of monastic foundations made in England at this period were in fact re-foundations of earlier establishments.[4] However, for now, 1018 will have to do.

The first Abbey was Benedictine. By comparison with the fifty or so

---

[1] A fragment of the Abbey's cartulary was discovered in 1897 and can be seen in the exhibition at Buckfast. It was about to be sold by an Exeter wastepaper merchant for making into children's drums!

[2] The Petre deeds and charters relating to Devon are now kept in the Devon Record Office. For further reference to this particular document, see also 'The Western Expansion of Wessex' by W.G.Hoskins, 1960.

[3] Malmesbury (c.960), Milton (c.964), Milton and Exeter (c. 965), Bath, Athelney and Muchelney (970), Cranborne (c. 980), Tavistock (981) and Sherborne (c.993): see Knowles, 'The Monastic Order in England', 1940.

[4] 'Excavations and Building Recording at Buckfast Abbey' (Devon Archaeological Society Proceedings, 1988) by S.W.Brown.

other abbeys in 11th century England, which together owned a sixth of the country, Buckfast was a 'small, unprosperous' house[5]. Its first monks probably came from Winchester or Tavistock, or from both these Abbeys. The rule of life which they adopted was that of the 'Regularis Concordia', drawn up at Winchester in about 970 for all Benedictine monasteries in England as part of the process of re-establishing monastic life, which had almost expired over the previous century.

We do not know where the Saxon monastery stood: a site nearer the river would possibly have been more convenient, considering the small size of the original abbey but, as today, there would have been the danger of flooding. It was probably wooden, although the church may have been made of stone. During the excavations of the 14th century Guest Hall a fragment of stone was discovered which may originally have been part of the Saxon church[6], but no other evidence of Aethelweard's monastery has been found, as yet.

To ensure its survival as a place of prayer, the founders of the little Saxon monastery endowed it with manors throughout the region. To get an idea of these endowments, we have to look at the 'Domesday Book' which, although drawn up in 1086, related to the state of things which existed 'on the day when King Edward (the Confessor) was alive and dead', i.e. in 1066. This was only 48 years after Buckfast's foundation, so that it prob-

ably represented the state of the Abbey and its possessions in their earliest form. There was the 'head of the Abbacy' itself, which is described as follows:

BUCKFAST ABBEY'S ENTRY IN THE DOMESDAY BOOK.

> *The abbot has a manor called BULFESTRA[7] [Exeter Domesday reading], and it is the seat of the Abbey and never paid geld. There the abbot has 1 smith and 10 serfs, who have 2 ploughs; there the abbot has also 3 swine, and woodland one league in length by one half league in width.*

This manor was only about 300 acres in size - about the same as the landed property of the present Abbey - but was supplemented by the proceeds from several other important manors (nearly 10,000 acres in all, with an annual revenue of £19 8s. 4d.) to the north (1), east (2) and south (3) of Dartmoor:

1. *a. Petrockstow* - lying in the bend of the Torridge. This is Heanton (old town) St. Petrock, as opposed to Newton St. Petrock, 7 miles west.

---

[5] Butler and Given-Wilson, 'Medieval Monasteries of Great Britain', 1979.

[6] See Appendix 2 of the Archaeological Report (Devon Archaeological Society Proceedings, 1988) by S.W.Brown.

[7] Only in the Exeter Domesday Book is the name 'Bulfestre' used for Buckfast, suggesting that it may have been a mistake by the scribe. Variations on the names 'Buckfast', 'Bocfast' or 'Bucfaesten', meaning 'the fastness, or stronghold, of the deer' (or of somebody called Buck) were used throughout the medieval period. The origin of the word should not be confused with 'Buckland', which derives from 'bocland', meaning 'land held by book or charter'.

    b. Aisse. Ash in Petrockstow in Shebbear hundred.

    c. Lymet. The monks' intake, hall or sele, commonly called Zeal Monachorum in North Tawton hundred.

    d. Dona. Down St. Mary in Crediton hundred.

2. *a. Trisma.* Trusham in Exminster hundred.

    b. Aisterona. In Ashburton in Teignbridge hundred.

3. *a. Aissa.* Abbot's Ash, alias Ashford in Aveton Giffard in Ermington hundred.

    b. Hetfeld. Heathfield in Aveton Giffard.

    c. Notona. Norton in Churchstow in Stanborough hundred.

    d. Cherforda. Charford in South Brent in Stanborough hundred.

    e. Brenta. South Brent Manor.

    f. Brenta. Great Aish in South Brent.

These lands sustained 92 villeins, 80 bordars (small farmers) and 67 serfs and their families. In all, 88 oxen, 80 goats, 29 pigs and 670 sheep were recorded by the Domesday surveyors. The large number of sheep point to what was an important source of revenue to Buckfast Abbey throughout the Middle Ages - the woollen industry.

We know from the Domesday Book that the Abbot in 1066 was Alwin. He attended a Shire-mote held in Exeter in about 1040, so we know he had been Abbot at least since then, but we are not certain that he was the Abbot in 1018; if so, he would have been in the 48th year of his abbacy by the Norman invasion - not impossible, but unusually long. If not, the name of the first Abbot of Buckfast has yet to be discovered.

The Norman invasion did not reach Devon until 1068, when William made a winter campaign to the West Country, suppressing a revolt based in Exeter and continuing to Totnes, where he gave the manor - together with 23,000 acres of land in the south and west of the county - to Juhel, one of his commanders. The Norman castles at Exeter and Totnes date from this campaign, and the Norman influence must soon have been felt, even though, unlike Tavistock Abbey, Buckfast was out of the limelight at this time.

For about fifty years after 1086, when the Domesday Book was written, Buckfast's history is obscure, but it seems likely that the house was in decline at this time, with two of its manors (Petrockstow and Aissa) temporarily under the management of the Bishop of Exeter. Henry I had confirmed the Abbey and its possessions at the beginning of his reign, but in 1136, when Stephen became king, radical action had to be taken to breathe life back into the monastery.

Stephen was sympathetic to monasteries, establishing and re-vitalising many of them during his reign (while in the country at large, civil war raged). Even before becoming king, Stephen had founded Furness, Neath, Quarr, Basingwerk, Stratford Langthorne and Buildwas Abbeys - all of them under the rule of the new, energetic Abbey of Savigny in southern Normandy. So it was that Buckfast was also given to the Abbot of Savigny, who chose a monk from his own community to lead a group across the Channel and establish the new Savignac rule at Buckfast[8]. Among other things, the Savignac observance added a new office (service) to the monastic horarium (daily cycle of offices): the Little Office of Our Lady. Also, instead of the traditional black habit, the monks wore grey habits (and were later known as

---

[8]The new Abbot's name was probably Eustace, whose signature is met with a few years later (1143) in a Totnes Deed.

'Grey Brothers'). We do not know how the remaining members of the Saxon community - if indeed there were any left by then - took to the new regime, but in the event this was only the precursor of a much more fundamental change: the transfer to the Cistercian Order only eleven years later in 1147.

The twelfth century was a time of extraordinary vigour throughout Europe. 'The epoch of the Crusades, of the rise of towns, and of the earliest bureaucratic states of the West, it saw the culmination of Romanesque art and the beginnings of Gothic; the emergence of the vernacular literatures; the revival of the Latin classics and of Latin poetry and Roman law; the recovery of Greek science, with its arabic additions, and much of Greek philosophy; and the origin of the first European universities'[9]. The twelfth century also saw the rapid rise of the Cistercian Order.

THE CISTERCIANS AT BUCKFAST

The reforms which led to the new order were started at the abbey of Cîteaux at the beginning of the century under the leadership of Abbot Stephen Harding, a native of Sherborne in Dorset. The Cistercian observance was conceived as a return to the Rule of St. Benedict in its original, austere form. The office now occupied six hours, and began with a service in the small hours of the morning. The elaboration of the Gregorian liturgy was replaced with a new simplicity. There were no hours of leisure. Shirts, bedspreads, robes, all luxuries were swept away. The churches were stripped of ornament; crucifixes were made of wood, not precious metal. New churches were built in a plain, undecorated style. The rule of silence was re-affirmed and a vegetarian diet enforced. The characteristic white Cistercian habits were made from natural, undyed wool.

The new Order encouraged a self-contained existence based on Prayer and Work - mostly on the Abbey's estates. Many of the new abbeys were set up in isolated and inhospitable places and, helped by the system of lay-brothers, who did the manual work, huge tracts of land were drained and improved for agricultural use, making 'two blades of grass grow where only one grew before'[10]. In England the Cistercian abbeys became well-known for their sheep farming - indeed the success of the wool trade in medieval England was largely due to them.

A MONK FROM MOUNT ST. BERNARD ABBEY, LEICESTER, ONE OF THE SMALL NUMBER OF CISTERCIAN MONASTERIES IN BRITAIN AND IRELAND TODAY.

The Cistercian Order's expansion was unprecedented: in the space of forty years 343 communities were established in Europe - 36 of them in England. The success of the Order was due to its greatest leader, St. Bernard, who went to Cîteaux as a novice in 1112 with 30 companions (among whom were his four brothers and uncle, apparently), before being sent to Cîteaux's daughter abbey at Clairvaux in 1115, where he later became abbot. The Cistercians were a centralised Order: the mother house established 'daughter' houses which could themselves set up new abbeys. Their

---

[9] Charles Homer Haskins, 'The Renaissance of the Twelfth Century', Meridian, 1957.

[10] J. Brooking-Rowe, 'Cistercian Houses of Devon', Transactions of the Devonshire Association, 8, p. 885, 1876.

underlying principle was the uniformity of observance. The abbot of a Cistercian monastery answered to the General Chapter - the annual meeting of the abbots from every monastery in the order. The meeting was chaired by the Abbot of Cîteaux, who was himself responsible to the Pope. Thus the Cistercian abbeys formed a network throughout Europe, free from local interference. It was at one meeting of the General Chapter, in 1147, that the whole Savignac group became affiliated to Cîteaux. In the official account St. Bernard's biographer, Godfrey, says:

'In this year was held the General Chapter, and none other presided than Pope Eugenius himself [Eugenius had previously been a Cistercian monk under St. Bernard]. *Therefore, all the abbots having gathered together as usual at Cîteaux, the aforesaid venerable Pope was present, not so much presiding by virtue of his apostolic authority, as assisting among them in paternal charity, as one of themselves.*

'Moreover, there was this special feature about this Chapter, which was without precedent, and was hardly to be hoped for: an entire and numerous congregation - an Order in itself, one should say - made up of more than 30 houses, scattered over France, England and Normandy - illustrious through its members, and not obscure through its churches and possessions, having given up its particular habit and institutions, which it had kept for many years, of its own accord adopted the rules and customs of Cîteaux, under the jurisdiction of Clairvaux.'

Thus it was that Buckfast became a Cistercian abbey in 1147. There was an immediate and fundamental transformation. The whole monastery was rebuilt in stone, in the Cistercian pattern. When the present monks returned to Buckfast in 1882, they were able to uncover almost all of the original foundations[11] and rebuild the abbey in the architectural style of the mid-twelfth century, so it is this original Cistercian abbey which has been restored. Archaeological excavations in the outer court (1982-1990) have shown that the whole precinct probably dates back to this period, with a range of buildings connecting the north and south gateways[12]. The arch of the north gate and part of a barrel-vaulted undercroft by the west cloister are now the only buildings to survive (above ground) from the original 12th century Cistercian abbey.

The Abbey's possessions were confirmed at the start of Henry II's reign in a charter which is of particular interest because it was witnessed by Thomas Becket, who was Chancellor at the time, before he became Archbishop of Canterbury. A few years later, in 1170, Thomas Becket was murdered in his cathedral by four knights, one of whom was Sir William de Tracy, owner of the manor of Bovey Tracey. Sir William is said to have built the church of St. Thomas at Bovey Tracey to atone for his deed.

During the reigns of Henry II's two sons, Richard I and John, national events had their impact on the Abbey. In 1193 Richard was captured and held to ransom by the Holy Roman Emperor, Henry VI, on his way back from the Third

---

[11] The excavations were carried out by the monks under the guidance of Dom Adam Hamilton, and a plan drawn up by Frederick Walters, the future architect for the restoration of the Abbey. A report of the excavations can be found in the 1884 Transactions of the Devonshire Association, vol. 16, pages 590 to 594, and in Dom Adam's 'History of Buckfast Abbey' (1906), pages 80 to 81. Both books are in the Abbey library. Sadly hardly anything has been saved from these excavations, although both the accounts mention tracery and large numbers of medieval tiles.

[12] The archaeological excavations of 1982-4 are written up in the Devon Archaeological Society Proceedings No. 46, 1988: 'Excavations and Building Recording at Buckfast Abbey, Devon', by S. W. Brown. Further excavations and surveying on the North Gate, part of the Guest Hall and the South Gate have not been published at the time of going to print, but information is available from the Archaeological Field Unit at Exeter Museum.

Crusade for the enormous sum of 150,000 marks (a mark was two thirds of a pound). He appealed to the nation for funds and the result was that all Cistercian monasteries had to give a year's supply of wool, which was already their main source of income. It was later agreed that the monks could commute the demand into a sum of money but nevertheless many monasteries ended up in debt as a result.[13]

TROUBLES UNDER KING JOHN

DESIGNS FROM SOME OF THE MEDIEVAL FLOOR TILES DISCOVERED AT BUCKFAST, NOW IN THE BRITISH MUSEUM.

When John came to the throne in 1199, the Cistercians must have looked forward to a period of royal favour: John was interested in theology and was well-disposed towards monasteries. He appointed the Abbot of Forde to be his chaplain and confessor, and Buckfast and Forde Abbeys were jointly entrusted with the safekeeping of the crown jewels for much of his reign.[14] However, this was merely the calm before the storm. In the event, King John's reign turned out to be almost as disastrous as that of Henry VIII was to be.

John's quarrels with Pope Innocent III over the election of the Arch-bishop of Canterbury led to the king seizing all the possessions of Canterbury and York, with the result that in 1208 the Pope imposed an Interdict. Effectively, this was a 'strike' by the country's priests, and it lasted for four years. No church services were allowed, including marriages and burials; sermons had to be given in the churchyard; there is even some doubt as to whether priests were allowed to administer the sacraments to the dying.

At first, Cistercian monasteries were exempted but after John was excommunicated in 1209 he turned on them with a vengeance and levied such huge sums from them that many were forced to close. At Buckfast, 'King John toke the seid abbay and all her landes and godes into his tenyure',[15] in other words he appropriated all the Abbey's rents, depriving it of its main source of income, which must have made it very hard to keep the monastery going. Nicholas, the Abbot of Buckfast, who guided his community through this difficult period, must have despaired. If the Abbey did close, the monks would probably have gone to live in other monasteries, but even there religious life must have been almost intolerable, with no services allowed. Furthermore, the people of England seem to have taken John's side against the Pope, and were extremely hostile to both secular and religious clergy. This can only have added to the trials endured by the monks at this time, until the Interdict was lifted in 1214.

---

[13] Richard was not sympathetic to the Cistercians: he is supposed to have said that 'of his three daughters, Covetousness, Pride and Lust, he would bestow the first upon the white monks', according to Brooking-Rowe, 'Cistercian Houses of Devon', 1876.

[14] This did not mean that the jewels were actually kept at Buckfast and Forde, simply that the abbeys carried the reponsibility for their safekeeping.

[15] Quoted from the Petre Estate papers by D. John Stéphan in 'A History of Buckfast Abbey', 1970, p. 67.

An artist's reconstruction of the abbey from the south-
west in the late Middle Ages, based on the surviving remains and
excavations of the church and cloister (1884) and the outer court (1982-
1991). The Cistercians were renowned for the orderly and uniform design of
their monasteries. Dominating the precinct was the church, with the conventual
buildings grouped around the cloister to the south. At the south-east corner was
the monks' infirmary. In general, areas to the east were more private and those to
the west more public. The abbot's lodging occupied a position at the south-west corner of the cloister, between the
private and public areas, reflecting his rôle as the Abbey's link with the outside world. To the west, the outer court
was bracketed by the gatehouses, which probably contained estate offices and manorial courts. Most of the buildings in the outer court at Buckfast were concerned with the needs of guests and visitors: besides the massive guest
hall and its south wing and kitchen, there were stables and a smithy, and further accommodation was provided for
distinguished guests in the abbot's lodging and for the poor in the almshouse attached to the south gate.

THE ABBEY AT ITS PEAK

After the troubles of the Interdict, Buckfast entered a long period of relative stability. A small chapel - possibly a Lady Chapel - was added at the eastern end of the church, and quantities of 13th century floor tiles, tracery and Purbeck marble columns excavated in the late 19th century indicate further building work in the cloisters, chapter house and refectory.

The 13th century was perhaps the period when the medieval Abbey was at its peak. Its represented a benign and civilising influence in the region with high standards of craftsmanship, building, farming, hygiene and of course learning.

The Abbey's cartulary was dispersed at the Dissolution along with the land holdings, rights and donations to which it related, but most of the surviving documents happen to come from this period and give an interesting picture of the Abbey's relationship with its close neighbours. As Dom Adam Hamilton, the Abbey's first historian writes, the charters 'are never dry or formal. The simple faith of the age often makes them often very beautiful. . . There is a picturesqueness, too, in the little annual acknowledgements which the knightly donors would require to keep alive the memory of their gifts. A pound of wax, to be presented on Assumption Day, was a favourite one; a red rose on the Feast of St. John the Baptist was another. One, a lady, must needs have a pair of white gloves at Michaelmas. Abbot Nicholas stipulates for a pound of pepper at Easter'.[16] In a charter of c.1240 Sir Robert de Helion granted to the Abbey an area of land at 'Hosefenne' (now Hawson Court) on the condition that the Abbot should use part of the income from the land to provide his monks (and surely also lay-brothers, employees and dependants!) with 64 gallons of wine on each of the four main feasts of Christmas, Candlemas, Pentecost and the Assumption, 'to be distributed in equal portions'. Another attraction of the 13th century charters is their place names, many of which, though changed, are still recognisable, seven centuries later: 'Hosefenne' (Hawson), 'Scoriaton' (Scoriton), 'Buddeton' (Button Farm), 'Leghe Bucfestre' (Buckfastleigh) and even 'Quercistede' (now 'Stumpy Oak', the Latin name for oak being 'quercus': probably the same oak tree, judging from its age).

A 13TH CENTURY RELIQUARY DOOR IN LIMOGES ENAMEL, DISCOVERED AT BUCKFAST.

WOOL FROM DARTMOOR

This was the time when the influence of the Cistercians made itself felt in the area, and in the country as a whole. As owners of large areas of land - land often in areas not extensively farmed before - the Cistercians became the country's main wool producers, setting up the industry which was to lead to England's great wealth in the later Middle Ages. In 1236 the Abbot and his monks were admitted to the guild of Totnes merchants. In 1315 Buckfast was listed

---

[16] 'A History of Buckfast Abbey', Dom Adam Hamilton, O.S.B., 1906.

THE BUCKFAST
ESTATE.
RENTS FROM
LANDHOLDINGS
PROVIDED THE
ABBEY WITH
MOST OF ITS
INCOME.

along with Forde, Newenham and Torre Abbey as an exporter of wool to Florence although it is likely that, in line with most abbeys in the country, Buckfast was sending wool to Italy by the end of the previous century. Many Italian merchants had come to England to act as agents for the collection of papal taxes, so they had all the right connections and were able to secure bulk deals from the monasteries. The wool probably went by ship to Italy, either via Totnes and Dartmouth, or through the abbey's own manor at Kingsbridge.

A Florentine dealer, author of 'La practica della Mercatura' (1340), had visited Devon to assess the quality and

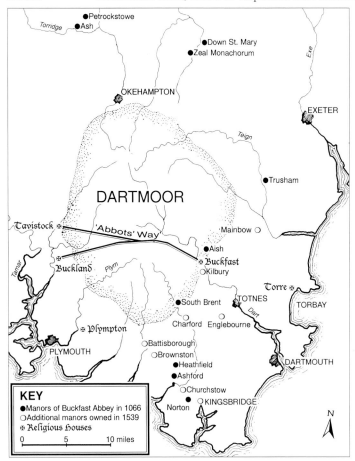

quantity of wool available from different monasteries. He wrote: 'At Ford Abbey, wool of good quality may be bought for 15 marks (£10) a sack (weighing 364 lbs. of wool), medium quality wool for 10 marks, and poorer for 9 marks. At Buckfast Abbey the range of prices ranges from $12\frac{1}{2}$ marks for the best wool, to 9 marks for the medium quality and 7 marks for the poorer sort and 10 sacks a year (the wool of some 2,500 sheep) may be had from Ford and Buckfast'.[17] The wool from Buckfast was presumably of poorer quality because the sheep were grazed on Dartmoor. 10 sacks weighed 1.6 tons and could have brought in up to £150 for the two abbeys. To put this income into perspective, Buckfast's total temporal income in 1291 was £42, and Forde's was £107.[18] Whether this figure included the income from wool is not known.

Some evidence of the farming activities of the Buckfast monks still survives. A short distance up the road from the North Gate is the Abbey's grange barn, now converted for residential use, where the monks would have threshed and stored their corn. On Dartmoor itself, another grange was excavated by Aileen Fox in 1956 on Dean Moor, before the area was flooded by the construction of the Avon dam.[19] This small homestead consisting of a small two-room house with a larger barn and an enclosed yard is described in a document

---

[17] Quoted by D. John Stéphan, *ibid.*.
[18] Quoted by David Knowles in 'Medieval Religious Houses of England and Wales', 1971.
[19] 'A Monastic Homestead on Dean Moor' by Aileen Fox, published in 'Medieval Archaeology', 1958.

of 1531 as a memorandum to a survey of moorland properties: the Abbey had kept a lay-brother 'in continual residence', with a shepherd to help him, until the time of the Black Death (1348-50). Fragments from about 20 rough cooking pots and pitchers were found, all dated between about 1250 and 1350, which would bear this out, although the small quantity of pottery and the small size of the accommodation might suggest a seasonal, rather than continuous use. The last lay-brother to live in this grange was 'frater Henricus Walbroke'. The woollen industry has remained an important part of Dartmoor life, with the Buckfast Spinning Company, next to the Abbey, still using Dartmoor wool - and water - for the production of carpet yarn.

AN ARTIST'S RECONSTRUCTION OF THE ABBEY'S GRANGE AT DEAN MOOR.

A FISHING DISPUTE

With the River Dart running close by, fishing was another important activity of the monks, as is shown by a colourful legal dispute. A deed of 1228 in the Cathedral Library at Exeter concerns the Fisheries of Staverton, owned by the Dean and Chapter of Exeter. The Abbot and Convent of Buckfast agree that the Dean and Chapter may operate fisheries there so long as they maintain an opening at least six feet wide for the free access of the fish upstream. In 1383 James and Thomas D'Audelegh, tenants of the manor of Dartington, complained to the Dean and Chapter because Abbot Robert Symons, together with seven monks and forty-four others (all named in the document), including the vicar of Holne, 'came armed to the Dean and Chapter's manor of Staverton, broke their closes, houses and the weirs of their two mills there and at Dertyngton, took their nets value £20 at Staverton, cut them into small pieces, felled their trees and underwood there, fished in their several fishery, carried off fish, trees and other goods, depastured their corn and grass, assaulted their servants, and so intimidated them that they dare not stay on their lands which remain uncultivated and uninhabited.' Presumably the D'Audeleghs had prevented fish from swimming upstream for such violent reprisals to have taken place. At about this time, the salmon taken from Staverton were valued at £40 a year by the Dean and Chapter, so the stakes were high. To receive a pardon for their crimes, the monks were fined £10 by the King and were required to pray daily for the D'Audelegh's souls and install their shields of arms in the windows of the Abbey church. Ironically a few years later in 1395 the Dean and Chapter gave the manor of Staverton Mill, together with its fisheries, to the monks of Buckfast Abbey, who held it until the Dissolution.[20]

---

[20] In 1537 the Abbot is recorded as sending a shipment of fish to the value of £50 to Thomas Cromwell - an indication of the economic importance of fishing to the Abbey throughout the Middle Ages. See page 19.

A ROYAL VISIT

Royal visits to the generally trouble-free West Country were very rare - only a dozen or so are recorded before 1800 - but in 1297 King Edward I came to the region to 'drum up' financial support for his French campaign. He travelled through Dorset in March and stayed at Forde Abbey on April 1st, at the Bishop's palace in Clyst on April 4th, at Exeter on the 5th, at Ilsington on Palm Sunday (April 7th), and at Buckfast Abbey from April 8th to 10th.[21] A Papal Bull of 1296 had forbidden the clergy to pay taxes to the king to aid his expeditions, and the king's response was to place them outside the law and seize their property. In the face of the king's formidable anger, however, hundreds of individual clergymen in Dorset and Devon took the opportunity of his visit to beg for pardon and ask for their property to be restored to them. He spent Easter at Plympton Priory, and from there he was able to oversee the naval preparations being made in Plymouth for his expedition.

THE GREAT SEAL OF KING EDWARD I.

In feudal times, English kings were constantly on the move around their country, taking with them a huge retinue with soldiers, servants, courtiers, advisors and family. At each place where they stayed, therefore, there had to be ample accommodation and food available, as well as a hall where trials, hearings and meetings could be conducted. It is possible that the Abbey's great Guest Hall[22] had been rebuilt in its final form by the time of Edward's visit, providing accommodation for many of the king's retinue, with the king himself probably staying in the Abbot's lodging. The meetings with local clergymen would have been held in the Chapter House.

THE BLACK DEATH

Fifty years after Edward I's visit, the Abbey - and indeed the whole country - was laid low by the Black Death, which arrived at Weymouth from Europe on July 7th 1348 and was at its height in Devon by about April of the following year. Abbot Stephen died at this time and was immediately succeeded by Abbot Philip. The next Abbot, Robert Symons, signed a charter in 1355 so it is possible that Abbot Philip had also died of the plague. The Abbots of Tavistock, Torre, and Hartland, and the Priors of St. James's and St. Nicholas's in Exeter, Barnstaple, Pilton, Minster, Modbury and St. Michael's Mount were all dead within six months. Many of the monks and lay-brothers must also have died: at Newenham Abbey only three were left alive out of twenty six; at Bodmin, only two survived. 28 years later, in 1377, there were still only 14 monks at Buckfast.[23] Episcopal records show that the secular clergy were being replaced at an alarm-

---

[21] D. John Stéphan, *ibid*, p. 102-103. For more detail see Henry Gough, 'The Itinerary of Edward I', 1900.

[22] The Guest Hall was excavated in 1983 and the archaeological evidence is fully written up in the Devon Archaeological Society Proceedings No. 46, 1988: 'Excavations and Building Recording at Buckfast Abbey, Devon', by S. W. Brown.

[23] Quoted by David Knowles in 'Medieval Religious Houses of England and Wales', 1971.

ing rate: at Ashburton there were four vicars in succession within three weeks. In March 1349 Bishop Grandisson appointed 60 new vicars in his Diocese; in April, 53; in May, 48; in June, 46; in July, 37. The decline in appointments might have been as much due to the dearth of replacement priests as to an abatement of the plague itself.

Excavations in the Outer Court between 1982 and 1990 may cast some light on the effects of the Black Death at Buckfast. Many of the buildings around the Abbey show signs that they either fell down or became disused in the mid 14th century, including the almshouse beside the South Gate, which appears to have burnt down, standing abandoned for many years before being re-roofed and used as a stable. The social necessity for an almshouse would have been reduced after the Black Death as housing was plentiful and, with labour in short supply, wages were high. The Abbey's disused buildings remained in this state for about thirty years, which was about as long as it took for the economy to recover.

Abbot Robert Symons, who was elected after the Black Death, is worth mentioning as he was the longest-serving of all Buckfast Abbots, before or since, holding the office for at least 40 years until 1395. He must have been an extremely robust and forceful man: besides surviving the plague and guiding his community through the lean period which followed, he was the leader of the party which raided the fisheries of Staverton (see page 11), as well as vigorously defending infringements on the Abbey's own property in other legal disputes. However, we may misjudge Abbot Robert if we label him as a belligerent, as the period after the Black Death was one of immense social upheaval, with unrest and lawlessness all over the country.

A WEALTHY LANDOWNER

The Cistercian abbey which had been launched with such a burst of energy in the middle of the 12th century had, by the 15th century, become a wealthy landowner and a pillar of the establishment. Nevertheless it had not lost sight of its social responsibilities, running its own guest hall, almshouse and alumnate[24] and maintaining its parishes and manors, establishing fairs and markets to encourage local trade.

To see how the Abbey took part in local affairs we can look at what was happening in Kingsbridge, its favourite manor in the late Middle Ages. The manor of Churchstow, which included the small fishing village of Kingsbridge, had been amongst the Abbey's earliest possessions, but it was not till the 15th century that Kingsbridge eclipsed its parent. By then the town was large enough to merit a complete rebuilding of the church, which was finished in 1414. The Abbot's house in Kingsbridge - or a rebuilding of it - also dated from this period; although the house has now disappeared, some wood panelling and carvings survive and have been re-used in the Abbot's throne at Buckfast. Also in

---

[24] An alumnate was a monastic school, providing a clerical education for boys whose parents wanted them to follow a religious career. Cistercians, unlike Benedictines, were not normally involved in education, but there is evidence that both Forde and Buckland Abbeys (both Cistercian) employed a lay teacher in the 1520s, and an amusing story - surely apocryphal - suggests that Buckfast may have had a school (Hamilton, ibid, p. 166). The Countess of Devon, walking near Hensleigh, met a tailor carrying a large basket. As she passed, she heard a cry from the basket and asked what was in it. 'Only seven puppies that I be going to drown in the Exe,' he replied. 'I want a dog;' said the Countess, 'open the hamper.' The tailor tried to excuse himself but the Countess insisted, and on the lid being raised, seven little babies were revealed. 'Alas! my Lady,' said the tailor, 'I am poor as a church mouse! My wife gave them to me all at once. What could I do but rid myself of them? See, they are all boys.' The Countess saw to their education, and when they were old enough sent them all to Buckfast Abbey, to be reared for the Church. Four became rectors of Tiverton, and the others their curates.

BUCKFAST'S TRADITIONAL LINKS WITH KINGSBRIDGE CONTINUE TODAY.

Kingsbridge was the 'Abbot's Mill' and two miles out at Norton, Buckfast had a farm.[25] In recent years the Abbey has renewed its historical links with Kingsbridge: the Abbot has been invited to attend the Kingsbridge Glove Fair in July and present the mayor with a copy of the fair charter (granted by Henry VI in 1461).[26]

The Abbot in the early years of the 15th century was William Slade, reckoned by some to have been the most distinguished of the Cistercian Abbots of Buckfast. Before becoming a monk he had had a fine academic career at Oxford, writing thirteen books and lecturing on Aristotle. He became a Fellow of Stapledon Hall (later Exeter College) in 1375, before being Vice-Rector in 1378 and Rector in 1380. As Rector he was responsible for building a new college library. In spite of being elected Rector for life, however, he gave up the office in 1385 and there are no further records of him at Oxford. It was at this time that he probably became a monk at Buckfast, a decision which Stéphan attributes to the ferment caused by the radical doctrines of John Wycliffe, a contemporary of Slade at Oxford. Fifteen years after coming to Buckfast, he was elected Abbot. While he will undoubtedly have improved Buckfast's standing as a centre of learning, he was also a builder. Besides the work in Kingsbridge, much of which probably dates from his abbacy, he is also credited with building work at Buckfast itself.[27] Hamilton's inspection of the foundations in 1884 made him 'strongly incline' to think that he rebuilt the north cloister, and stonework discovered at the base of the church tower at this time also show that it was rebuilt in the 15th century. More recently, archaeologists have dated the complete rebuilding of the South Gate and its attached range to this period. William Slade died in 1415.

AN ABBOT IN TROUBLE

The Abbots of Buckfast in the 15th and 16th centuries were elected for life, and were in personal control of a huge concern, with manors and business interests all over Devon, never mind the spiritual well-being of their monks. It

[25] Besides the manor at Norton, which was recorded as the property of Buckfast in the Domesday Book, many people have argued that the Abbey also owned Leigh Barton, a medieval farm with several grand 15th century additions, two miles from Norton. Leigh Barton was described by Beric Morley in the Devon Archaeological Society Proceedings, no. 41, 1983, p. 81-106. There is no documentary evidence for Leigh having belonged to Buckfast Abbey - in fact a family called Leigh seems to have held the freehold from the 13th to the 17th century - but Morley argues that there may have been an informal connection with Buckfast in the 15th century. Many historians disagree with Morley on the grounds that any substantial connection with Buckfast would certainly have appeared in the documentary evidence. However, Leigh is such a fine medieval building that some people are reluctant to accept that Buckfast Abbey had no connection with it!

[26] Fairs and markets were also established by the Abbey at its manors of South Brent (1353) and Buckfastleigh (1461).

[27] The 16th century writer and antiquarian, John Leland, visited Buckfast both before and after the Dissolution in 1539. On his first visit he found out about William Slade and said, 'He is the only man, wherever we turn, who added lustre to this monastery. His memory is still fresh among them even to this day (i.e. 120 years later), as is proved by the buildings he erected and the books he wrote. For he wrote: Universalia super libros Physicorum; Quaestiones de anima; Super Sententias; Flosculos moralium.' Quoted in D. John Stéphan, ibid., p. 132.

must have been hard for some monks to make the change from the more cloistered way of life to this position of power. Abbot William Slade seems to have been eminently suitable for the job but his successor, William Beaghe, was not so illustrious. He was the only Abbot who lost the confidence of his community, with the result that in 1421 the monks complained to Cîteaux, stating (delicately, in view of later revelations!) that discord had arisen between the Abbot and his community 'concerning the government and administration of the abbey in spiritual and temporal matters . . . and concerning other causes, points and articles, which at the present moment it would be too tedious to relate' and suggests that the Abbot should be suspended, but could remain at the Abbey in retirement with a pension, servants and a number of privileges. A Visitor would be appointed to assess the accusations.

However, this complaint was not resolved and in 1423 the matter was taken to Rome. This time the accusations are more specific: the Abbot 'has begotten children by divers women whom he keeps as concubines; has granted away to divers persons for life without the consent of the Convent a number of possessions and tenements, and divers pensions of the monastery; has alienated certain of its precious movables and given them to the said women and children, and that by his negligence the monastery is greatly collapsed and certain of the monks have thrown off the observance of the Rule and wander forth; that the divine worship is sadly neglected to the detriment of their souls and the scandal of many persons.'[28] The Abbots of Beaulieu and St. Mary Graces (London) were appointed as Visitors; they recommended that Abbot Beaghe be suspended and that the Prior, Thomas Rogger, should govern the Abbey during his lifetime and then succeed him as Abbot. In the event Beaghe resigned in 1432; we do not know the date of his death. If this had happened a century later, the whole affair would have taken on a political significance, as Henry VIII looked for evidence of corruption in the monasteries to justify his decision to close them down.

A HAZARDOUS JOURNEY TO THE GENERAL CHAPTER

One feature of the 15th century was a marked deterioration in the conditions of travel in Europe. With its mother house in Burgundy, European travel was a fact of life for the Cistercian order; there was frequent correspondence, and the General Chapter was held at Cîteaux every year. However, during the Hundred Years' War and afterwards, as European countries became more nationalistic, it became increasingly dangerous to travel. Most English Cistercian abbeys were not able to comply with an order that their abbots should attend General Chapter meetings, and in 1471 Abbot John Kyng of Buckfast was asked by 33 other English abbots to choose a representative to act as their proxy. He chose Lazarus de Padway, an ecclesiastical lawyer, who has left a fascinating account of his nightmare journey to and from Cîteaux. 'I can hardly describe the hazards and dangers we had to endure during this journey,' he wrote in a letter to Abbot Kyng. 'As a number of your fellow-Abbots were making their way from Germany to the General Chapter, though they were supplied with safe conducts by the king of France and the Dukes of Burgundy and Lorraine, they were nevertheless molested by robbers in the very church of your monastery of Morimond, carried off in fetters and cast into prisons: their horses, valued at 24 gold pieces, and money amounting to 500 Rheims florins, were all taken from them.' When he arrived, he discovered that the Abbot of Cîteaux himself was ill, recovering from a similar attack on a recent

---

[28] Quoted by D. John Stéphan, ibid., p. 148 from the Lateran Regesta, Vol. CCXXXIV.

journey. After conducting his business in Cîteaux, Lazarus de Padway began his return journey but discovered that the borders had just been closed between France and Burgundy. He lacked a safe conduct, and both the King of France and the Duke of Burgundy were about twelve days' journey away. As illegal immigrants were to be imprisoned, he 'followed the most circuitous routes, across mountains and forests, riding by night rather than by day under grievous difficulties' until he reached Rheims, where the Constable of France gave him a safe conduct to Flanders. He even ran into a 'raging tempest' crossing the channel! 'I take my oath on it, most Reverend Father, that were I to live for centuries, I would not care to repeat such a journey, with such perils and fatigues - not for ten marks, or even a hundred pounds at a time like this.'[29] Lazarus de Padway's account may read more like the adventures of Baron Münchausen, but it does illustrate how Europe was losing the cohesion that it had in the early Middle Ages.

Abbot Kyng was similar in some ways to Abbot William Slade. In 1460, as Prior of Buckfast, he was appointed by the General Chapter in Cîteaux to the post of Provisor ('the head, guardian, director and rector'[30]) of the Cistercians' college in Oxford, St. Bernard's (later St. John's). However, four years later the college obviously complained to Cîteaux that Kyng was spending too much time at Buckfast: he was warned that he would be replaced as Provisor if he did not mend his ways. He must have complied with the order because he remained at Oxford until 1467 when he left for good to become Abbot of Buckfast - a post he was to hold for thirty years. There is very little documentary evidence of him, but like Abbot Slade he was a builder. He may have rebuilt the Chapter House,[31] and two of the most impressive medieval buildings still standing at Buckfast probably date from his abbacy - both of them illustrating the Abbey's changing relationship with society in the late 15th century.[32] The south wing of the Guest Hall, which has survived

THE SOUTH WING OF THE ABBEY'S GUEST HALL, FULLY RESTORED IN 1992.

almost unchanged and was restored to its original appearance in 1992, has a grand first floor hall with store-rooms on the ground floor. The Abbey already had considerable facilities for guests from all levels of society: the almshouse next to the South Gate for the poorest vagrants, the main Guest Hall for the majority of travellers and the Abbot's lodging for the most important visitors. This new hall was for daytime use only; it had no access into the Guest Hall itself, but was reached by a grand external staircase conveniently close to the guest hall kitchen: it was probably a kind of medieval 'function room' for laity using the Abbey, where meetings could be held and parties fed and entertained.

The other building which probably dates from Abbot Kyng's term

---

[29] The whole letter is printed in D. John Stéphan, ibid., p. 166-171. He translated it from a document discovered in the Archives of Cîteaux in Dijon.

[30] From the Statutes of the Cistercian General Chapters, Vol V, quoted in Stéphan, ibid., p. 164-5.

[31] Most of the finds from the 1884 excavations in the area of the Chapter House (shafts, tracery, statuary, etc.) were late 15th century in date.

[32] Lionel Butler and Chris Given-Wilson's 'Medieval Monasteries of Great Britain', 1979, p. 72-93, has a good account of the secularisation of the monasteries from the 13th century onwards, including the replacement of lay-brothers by servants, the separation of the abbot from his community and the change from farmer to landlord.

of office is the 'Abbot's Tower' at the south-western corner of the conventual buildings. This was a series of three small but very well-appointed rooms adjoining the western range, which had by then probably changed from the lay-brothers' accommodation to the Abbot's private lodgings. Each room had the luxury of its own fireplace and garderobe en suite, suggesting that the 'Abbot's Tower' was probably for the Abbot's most important guests.

With the 'Abbot's Tower' and the new south wing, Abbot Kyng was responding to what was for the larger monasteries an increasing rôle in the later Middle Ages: providing hospitality for the growing number of people travelling around the country. This put a considerable financial strain on some monasteries, besides bringing luxury into the precinct. Although the Benedictine Rule encouraged hospitality, it was never intended to be on such a scale and was in some ways a distraction from the original purpose of the monasteries.

GATHERING CLOUDS

By the beginning of the 16th century the monasteries, although very rich, were in decline. In the 13th century there had been some 20,000 monks and nuns in the country, amongst a population of three million; by 1500 there were only 12,000 - one monk per 250 lay people in the population. At Buckfast in the 12th century there may have been as many as 60 choir monks and perhaps twice as many lay-brothers; between 1500 and 1539, only 22 monks were ordained, ten of whom remained at the Dissolution and signed the deed of surrender.[33] Meanwhile this diminishing number of monks and nuns owned perhaps as much as a quarter of the whole country, with the rents from their estates making up two thirds of their income and only three per cent of it spent on charity for the sick and poor.[34] Their rôle as centres of learning had been taken over by the universities, and the number of secular hospitals and inns was increasing at the expense of those run by monasteries.[35] The writing was on the wall.

Dissolutions were not new. During the Hundred Years' War against France, Edward I, II and III had closed many of the priories with mother houses in France, with the remaining hundred of them being closed by Henry V. So when Henry VIII, as the 'Supreme Head of the Church of England', turned his mind to the Dissolution, he would have been able to find at least some historical justification for his actions. Henry needed to know the value of each monastery so in 1535 he asked local commissioners to carry out the *Valor Ecclesiasticus*, the most detailed survey of ecclesiastical property since William the Conqueror's Domesday Book.

In 1535 Henry VIII appointed a new Vicar General, Thomas Cromwell, with instructions to visit and reform the houses of the religious orders. Only a year later, the smaller monasteries in England (those with a value of less than

THE LATE 15TH CENTURY 'ABBOT'S TOWER'.

---

[33] Cromwell's visitors in 1535 had 'released' monks who had been professed when under age. Joyce Youings, 'The Dissolution of the Monasteries', 1971.

[34] Figures from the (admittedly partial) *Valor Ecclesiasticus* of 1535. See D. Knowles, 'The Religious Orders in England', Vol. 3, 1959, p. 264-266 for a fuller discussion of the charitable work of the abbeys at this time.

[35] Some monasteries had actually been dissolved in the 15th century in order to use their income to found university colleges. St. John's College, Cambridge and Magdalen College, Oxford were founded in this way, and the chantry and hospital at Windsor were founded by Henry VII by diverting the monastic properties of Luffield Priory.

THE
ARCHITECTS
OF THE
DISSOLUTION
OF BUCKFAST
ABBEY: THOMAS
CROMWELL
(RIGHT) AND
WILLIAM PETRE,
THE LAWYER
WHO HANDLED
THE CLOSURE
AND WHO LATER
BOUGHT THE
ABBEY'S TWO
LARGEST
MANORS.

£200) had been closed down, with this essentially financial decision justified on the grounds that they were centres of 'manifest sin, vicious, carnal and abominable living' - a conclusion not supported by the Visitors' reports. Two revolts against Henry VIII's rule - the 'Pilgrimage of Grace' and the Lincolnshire Rebellion - were ruthlessly suppressed, and a number of monks hanged.[36] Having made this example, Cromwell's commissioners found it easy to secure the voluntary agreement of nearly all the monasteries to their closure. Added to this veiled threat, co-operative monks and abbots were offered generous pensions. Even so, it is surprising that there was so little opposition to the Dissolution, either from the country or from the monasteries themselves or their tenants. There are very few records of force being used to close a monastery; in almost every case the monks or nuns simply signed their home over to the king's commissioners. By 1540 all of them - some 850 in total - had been closed, and the king was richer by £165,000 a year.

The suppression of Buckfast Abbey was a particularly shabby affair. Until 1535 there had been an unbroken line of Abbots chosen by the monks from their own community; now, at this final stage, an Abbot was intruded. His appointment so soon before the Dissolution makes it hard not to conclude that he was given the brief of overseeing the winding down and closure of the Abbey.[37]

The new Abbot, Gabriel Donne, was a native of Devon and a Cistercian monk of Stratford Langthorne Abbey in Essex. In 1535, masquerading as a theology student, he assisted one Harry Philipps in an undercover expedition to Flanders to entice William Tyndale, the exiled reformer and opponent of Henry VIII, from his home and hand him over to the authorities, who executed him. It seems unlikely that they were acting on the orders of Cromwell or the king himself, who would not have become involved in a potentially embarrassing international incident, but as Donne was related by marriage to Cromwell - in 1517 his niece had married Cromwell's nephew - and had probably known him for many years, Cromwell may have been involved. Certainly, as a result of the success of the expedition, Donne was

[36] The Abbot of Colchester was one of the victims, and by a long and roundabout route his pectoral cross is now at Buckfast Abbey. It is a fine gilded and enamelled Italian piece, and is on loan from the Clifford family (see pages 24-25) until such time as Colchester Abbey should be refounded as a Benedictine Abbey.

[37] Most historians (e.g. Knowles, Butler, Youings) question, however, whether the Dissolution of the greater monasteries was planned from the start by Henry VIII or Cromwell; the ease with which the lesser monasteries succumbed in 1536 seems to have encouraged them to continue in the same vein. Thus Donne may in fact have seen his appointment to the abbacy as a lifelong one. This view is *not* supported by Stéphan.

rewarded: 'within this five or six weeks he is come to London and by Mr. Secretary's (i.e. Cromwell's) help has obtained an abbey of 1000 marks in the West Country.'[38]

Donne's continuing good relationship with Cromwell is perhaps the most telling indication of his collusion in the Dissolution of his own Abbey and his disregard for his promise, on becoming Abbot, to safeguard the interests of his community. We have evidence of the close ties between the two men in a letter of 1537 from a Harry Huttoft to Thomas Cromwell describing how a fisherman 'bringing fish for your Lordship from the Abbot of Buckfast' was attacked by French pirates and 'robbed to the value of 50L.'

An indication of the progress towards dissolution is clear from the number of alienations of the Abbey's property: between 1481 and 1535 there were 25 such transactions, compared with 53 in the four years of Donne's abbacy. Donne also took the trouble to confirm the annuities and pensions of some of the Abbey's lay employees, including the chief steward,[39] Sir Thomas Dennys (who subsequently bought the Abbey itself at the Dissolution, and who later married Donne's sister Elizabeth) and the steward, John Southcote, who were granted annual incomes of £6 13s. 4d. and 53s. 4d. respectively for life.

THE DISSOLUTION

The fateful day arrived on 25th February 1539. The king's commissioners, led by a select group of some five distinguished lawyers, had been travelling around the country for the past twelve months closing monasteries as they went. Two of them, William Petre and John Tregonwell, turned their attention to the West Country in January 1539, starting in Wiltshire and reaching Somerset by the beginning of February. In Exeter they separated in order to 'clean up' the remaining eight monasteries in Devon and Cornwall: Petre was at Torre on 23rd and Buckfast on 25th, before continuing to Buckland (27th) and Plympton Priory (March 1st). They met

BUCKFAST ABBEY'S DEED OF SURRENDER, NOW HELD IN THE PUBLIC RECORD OFFICE IN LONDON.

---

[38] Quoted by D. John Stéphan, *ibid.*, p. 204 from a letter from Thomas Tebolde to the Archbishop of Canterbury now in the State Papers of Henry VIII, 1535. Dom Adam Hamilton suggests that the previous Abbot, John Rede, was expelled to make way for Gabriel Donne: 'Abbot Rede would naturally apply to the Bishop of Exeter for a benefice. A few months after the intrusion I find a John Rede vicar of Davidstowe in Cornwall' (p. 265).

[39] A very important post in the late Middle Ages, acting as the representative of the Abbey in all civil matters and in the manorial courts.

again in Dorset on March 8th to close Forde Abbey. In just four months, these two men - accompanied no doubt by various clerks, guards and a pack-horse train - visited and closed forty monasteries. During each brief visit they will have presented and witnessed the signing of the Deed of Surrender, assigned pensions to the monks and taken possession of the Abbey's seals, charters and church plate; after this particular campaign they delivered $1\frac{1}{2}$ tons of gold, gilt and silver to the Tower of London, which included the treasures of Buckfast Abbey.[40]

William Petre will have conducted his business in the Chapter House,[41] with the Abbey's stewards, Sir Thomas Dennys and John Southcote probably also present. Abbot Gabriel Donne received the huge pension of £120 a year, the Prior £8 and the remaining nine monks between £5 and £6. As for what happened to the monks after the Abbey had been closed, Gabriel Donne was made Prebendary of St. Paul's in London, as well as being given the rectory of Stepney as a sinecure. Five of the remaining monks found employment in local parishes, perhaps as priests or chaplains. Of the others, there is no information.

SHARING THE SPOILS

The total net revenues of Buckfast Abbey were £466 11s. 2d.[42] The Abbey's lands became the king's property and tenancy agreements did not change to any great extent; for most people the Dissolution merely meant a change of landlord. However, during the next few years some of the Abbey's manors were bought from the king - all by people who had been present at the signing of the Dissolution charter and could expect preferential treatment. William Petre himself bought the largest and most prosperous manors of South Brent in 1545 and Churchstow (near Kingsbridge) in 1555.[43] John Southcote, the steward, bought the manor of Trusham in 1540. The manor of Buckfast itself, including the Abbey, was rented immediately by the chief steward, Sir Thomas Dennys, and bought outright in 1540 for £314 15s. whereafter it became known as 'Buckfast-Dennys'. The manor was to remain in the Dennys family for 250 years.

The Abbey was immediately vacated and demolition work started on the buildings. Lead was melted down,[44] furniture and movables were auctioned and the Abbey's five bells were bought by the parishioners of Buckfastleigh for

---

[40] This delivery also included 'superfluous plate' from Wells, Exeter and Salisbury Cathedrals. See F.G.Emmison, 'Tudor Secretary - Sir William Petre at Court and Home', 1961, p. 12-16 for a full account of the West Country dissolutions in 1539.

[41] The Chapter House was in the eastern range of the cloisters, on the site of the present sacristy. Dom Adam Hamilton who conducted the excavations of the site in 1884, used his knowledge to describe the setting in detail - a good piece of secondary evidence in view of the fact that so little has survived from these excavations. He mentions three inscribed tombstones of abbots, bright green and yellow tiles and a low bench of red sandstone around the walls. 'A History of Buckfast Abbey', 1906, p. 208-9. One stone coffin was kept and is now in the Abbey's exhibition.

[42] The text of the Deed of Surrender, with a summary of the spiritual and temporal revenues of the Abbey is described in D. John Stéphan, *ibid.*, p. 216-230.

[43] Ironically, having presided over the closure of Buckfast Abbey, William Petre and his decendants continued to play a part in its history - and in the re-establishment of monastic life there. The family became supporters of Roman Catholicism and in the early years of the 20th century Lady Petre lived close to Buckfast in a house called 'The Rosary' and donated a ring to Abbot Bruno Fehrenbacher as part of his official insignia.

[44] It appears that most of the roofs at Buckfast were slated, probably even the church. An interesting angle on this is provided in an account commissioned in 1549 in response to Lord Russell demanding ammunition to put down the Western Rebellion. The account lists the amounts of lead obtained from the Devon monasteries, most of which were covered with 'Sclatt & Tyle'. Buckfast was supposed to have provided 'vi fooders' (about a ton) of lead, but this was disputed by Sir Thomas Dennys, who said that the only lead that came from Buckfast was from guttering, and that he would pay £100 per 'fooder' if he was proved wrong - which he was not. How shocked the monks would have been if they had known that the lead from their abbey was to be made into bullets to shoot Catholics! See 'Lead from the Dissolved Religious Houses in Devon in 1549' by Frances Rose-Troup in 'Devon & Cornwall Notes and Queries' Vol. XIX (1936-7), p. 125.

£33 15s.[45] Archaeologists working on the site of the Guest Hall discovered what might have been a temporary wooden crane, perhaps used to dismantle the massive roof timbers; certainly the job of demolishing the larger Abbey buildings must have been formidable. It seems that the church and conventional buildings were stripped and left to decay, but many of the smaller buildings in the Outer Court were retained and converted for different uses. The 'Long Chamber' - probably the almshouses beside the South Gate - were put to some light industrial use, perhaps wool dyeing, judging from some large stone vats which were installed at that time. The 'house ower the South yeate' was rented by a John Weldon for 4s. Richard Bennett held 'the greate Hall' - presumably the Guest Hall and its associated buildings - and set about converting them to a farm. The Guest Hall itself was partly demolished and became a line of cottages and a barn, with a farmyard in the shelter of the massive ruinous walls. The south wing was converted for use as a farmhouse - 'Abbey Farm' - and remained largely unchanged for the next 400 years.

AFTER THE DISSOLUTION THE GREAT 14TH CENTURY GUEST HALL BECAME A FARM - 'ABBEY FARM'.

BUCKFAST WITHOUT THE ABBEY

Tracing the history of Buckfast for the two centuries following the Dissolution is difficult. The Dennys family never lived at Buckfast, so information about their activities is hardly relevant to the history of the Abbey. The archaeology of the buildings in the former Outer Court shows that they remained largely the same until the early 19th century: Buckfast was a small rural hamlet - much smaller than Buckfastleigh - with some minor industry related to the wool trade.

The earliest illustration of the Abbey ruins dates from 1734 (see page 22), when the brothers Samuel and Nathaniel Buck included Buckfast in their series of engravings of historic sites. The only parts still in use at this time are the North and South Gates, which are arched and roofed. Of the conventual buildings, the Abbot's Tower is visible with a tall gable adjoining it, possibly belonging to the Abbot's lodging. In the foreground is a building in the right position and with the right proportions to be the Refectory. The church must have almost disappeared by this time.

In about 1760 Jeremiah Milles, Dean of Exeter, made a plan of the remains as well as sketches of the Abbey's two gatehouses, now roofless and uninhabited. He described the North Gate as having 40 feet of mural paintings, as well as pedestrian passages either side of the main thoroughfare. Milles' drawing of the South Gate may in fact be our best evidence of the original archway, before it was moved to its present position in the 18th or 19th century to make way for an expanding woollen mill on the site.

---

[45] The Abbey's bells remained in Buckfastleigh parish church until in was burnt down in July 1992 by arsonists. The bells were temporarily returned to the Abbey for safe-keeping while the parish church tower was being repaired.

ABOVE: THE RUINS OF BUCKFAST ABBEY IN 1734 BELOW: THIS NEO-GOTHIC MANSION WAS BUILT ON THE SITE IN 1806.

Even as late as 1793, when Rev. John Swete visited Buckfast, the ruins were still very much in evidence: 'disparted fragments encumber a large spot of ground, the cement of which being harder than the stones which it has connected together hath rendered every attempt to remove them so expensive that they have lain for a century and will probably remain for a century more.' However, he was to be proved wrong, for in 1800 the 'old walls' were bought by Samuel Berry, owner of the tucking mill by the South Gate, and most of the rubble was cleared away to make way for his neo-Gothic mansion, completed in 1806. Berry retained the Abbot's Tower as a folly and kept the 12th century undercroft as

a cellar, but the rest of the Abbey was flattened. Contemporary engravings and paintings show how much the view altered in those few years.

Meanwhile the village of Buckfast had been developing into a small but thriving industrial community: two mills - Higher Mill and Berry's Mill - produced serge and blankets for military and colonial use and provided employment for most of the villagers. Several lines of terraced houses clustered around Berry's Mill and the medieval South Gate - known then as 'the Barracks' because so many people lived there. Although there was no pub in the village, workers met at lunch breaks in the barn of 'Abbey Farm' (through the main arched entrance to the original Guest Hall) which served as a Cider House (cider orchards being another major feature of the area at that time). Near the 12th century North Gate a Methodist Chapel was built in 1881.[46]

As for Samuel Berry's mansion, standing in its park behind a high wall, it changed hands four times over the next eighty years. Berry had overstretched himself, and in 1825 he went bankrupt and the Buckfast estate[47] became the property of William Searle Benthall, whose family owned it until 1872, when it was bought by Dr. James Gale. Ten years later Dr. Gale himself decided to sell the property, but was keen to offer it to a religious community.[48] A friend wrote a letter to 'The Tablet' on his behalf on September 6th 1882, describing the Abbey and recommending it as 'a grand acquisition could it be restored to its original purpose.' The effect was almost instantaneous: six weeks later monks were again living at Buckfast Abbey, after a gap of 343 years.

MONKS RETURN TO BUCKFAST

The monks who arrived at Buckfast in 1882 had come by a very roundabout route, starting from the monastery of La Pierre-qui-Vire, which had been founded by Père Jean-Baptiste Muard in 1849 in the middle of a forest in the Morvan region of central France. La Pierre-qui-Vire later joined the Subiaco Congregation of Benedictine monasteries. In 1880 the French government sent out orders to suppress all 'unauthorised' religious houses in the country and on November 5th of that year a party of soldiers and *gendarmes* arrived at La Pierre-qui-Vire, where they had to break in the doors of the monastery to evict the monks. Having broken in they discovered that each monk had locked himself in his own room, so that every cell door had to be broken down as well! Eventually the monks were evicted and had to disperse. One group, under the leadership of Père Thomas Dupérou, made its way to England. They were given shelter by the Benedictine monks of St. Augustine's Priory (later Abbey) in Ramsgate, who owned a large property - once an agricultural college - at Leopardstown on the outskirts of Dublin. As none of the French monks could speak English, one of the Ramsgate monks, Dom Adam Hamilton, agreed to accompany them to Ireland where they landed on November 28th 1880 - only three weeks after leaving La Pierre-qui-Vire.

THE RETURNING BUCKFAST COMMUNITY IN 1882.

---

[46] The local history of Buckfast is very well described and illustrated in 'Buckfast in Bygone Days', by Hilary Beard, 1991.

[47] In the late 19th century, besides the mansion, the estate consisted of about sixteen acres of land, the ruinous 'Abbot's Tower', a cottage adjoining the 12th century North Gate arch and a farmhouse - now the Abbey's offices. Although the Benthalls owned other properties at Buckfast, such as the cottages and farmhouse on the site of the medieval guest hall, these were not sold to Dr. Gale or to the returning monks - indeed, the monks did not purchase any of the outer parts of the original precinct until the 1980s. At the time of writing, the Methodist Chapel near the North Gate is the only building within the original medieval precinct which is not owned by the Abbey.

[48] Dr. Gale was a 'blind inventor' of, among other things, a substance for making gunpowder inactive. He was not only sympathetic to Catholics: he also laid the foundation stones of the Wesleyan Chapel in Dartmouth and the Greenbank Bible Christian Chapel in Plymouth.

The small community - about 30 altogether - stayed in Leopardstown for two years, but they were living on Ramsgate's charity, so were looking for suitable properties in Ireland throughout this time. It was then that Dom Adam Hamilton noticed the letter in 'The Tablet'. Père Dupérou was very excited and he immediately travelled with Dom Adam to Plymouth, where they met Dr. Gale, saw Buckfast Abbey and immediately took out a lease on it, with the intention to proceed with a purchase at a later date. The first six monks arrived at Buckfast on 28th October 1882, with the remainder of the community following during the next few weeks. Eight months later they bought the Abbey from Dr. Gale for £4,700.[49]

Straight away there was public interest and support for the monks and Dom Adam Hamilton organised a committee to help the monks with their plans to restore the Abbey. The chairman was Lord Clifford, of Ugbrooke near Chudleigh, and the members included Cardinals Manning and Newman, the Duke of Norfolk and a number of other Lords, Bishops and Knights. They appointed Mr. Frederick A. Walters as architect - the beginning of a long and fruitful relationship covering nearly fifty years, and continuing with his son until the whole project was complete.

THE FOUNDATIONS OF THE ORIGINAL ABBEY WERE DISCOVERED IN 1884.

Frederick Walters was one of the leading architects of his day. As a member of the Society of Antiquaries, his research was impeccable and his attention to detail extraordinary. He became involved with every aspect of the revival of the Abbey, designing furnishings, sculptures, coats-of-arms and vestments, as well as providing plans for several houses and the local primary school in the years that followed.

Using the evidence of the Buck print of 1734 (see page 22) and the few ruins still standing, Walters drew up a plan for the restoration of the Abbey. This first plan turned out to be completely wrong: he must have mistaken the substantial ruins in the foreground of the print for the church, which he placed to the south of the conventual buildings, in a 15th century style to fit in with the Abbot's Tower.

THE ANCIENT FOUNDATIONS UNCOVERED

Shortly after Walters had made his proposal, one of the monks discovered the real foundations of the medieval monastery, apparently while digging the garden to the north of the mansion.[50] Straight away the monks - under the

---

[49] Dr. Gale had himself purchased the Abbey in 1870 for £3,500; he must have been well satisfied with the profit!

[50] Accounts vary about how the foundations were discovered. One states that a stonemason working on the restoration the Abbot's Tower noticed what he guessed were the regular lines of the foundations showing as patches of yellow grass during the hot summer of 1883, and brought them to the attention of Frederick Walters. Br. Paul Lascaraboura chanced upon the actual foundations in the autumn of that year, and shortly afterwards Walters accompanied Br. Paul around the site with a crowbar, 'sounding out' the full ground plan. All three accounts have at different times been claimed as the first discovery. See 'Buckfast Abbey Chronicle', 1937, p. 185.

guidance of Frederick Walters, Dom Adam Hamilton and Mr. J. Brooking Rowe - uncovered the rest of the foundations, revealing what was almost certainly the complete 12th century ground plan of the Cistercian abbey.[51] By March 1884 Walters had made accurate drawings of the foundations and put forward another design for the rebuilding of the Abbey in the style of the mid-12th century, based on studies of abbeys such as Kirkstall and Fountains.

BONIFACE NATTER, FIRST ABBOT OF THE RESTORED MONASTERY.

Meanwhile the fund-raising committee had been working hard and the monks had been able to pay for the restoration of the Abbot's Tower and the construction of a temporary church (now the Chapter House) next to it: this was opened on 25th March 1884. Also in 1884, work started on the South Wing, including the kitchen, refectory and cloister, mostly paid for by Lord Clifford himself; he was later to give funds for the east cloister and his nephew the north cloister. As an indication of the close relationship between the Clifford family and the Abbey, Lady Clifford was the only woman to be granted the rare privilege of entering the enclosure of the monastery whenever she visited Buckfast.[52]

During this time, conditions had improved in France and La Pierre-qui-Vire was again a 'going concern', with the Buckfast monks still officially part of the community; it was not until 1899 that Buckfast was given independent status and not until 1902 that it finally became an Abbey again. The first Abbot to be elected was Dom Boniface Natter, from southern Germany, who had joined the community at La Pierre-qui-Vire at the age of 12 as an *alumnus* just before it was evicted. As the original French monks at Buckfast became older, Abbot Boniface looked to his native Swabia, where there were no monasteries, for new 'recruits'. He was soon able to fill the alumnate (a small school) with Catholic boys, about half of whom went on to be priests or monks. Apart from Dom Adam Hamilton, it was not until after the First World War that British monks began to come to Buckfast in any number.

Life at Buckfast in the early years was very strict, a legacy from the Abbey's origins in La Pierre-qiu-Vire where the monks, although Benedictines, followed what was in effect a Trappist way of life. The 2.00 a.m. night office was retained until 1933; silence was strictly observed in the monastery (leading to the habitual use of sign-language); monks knelt when speaking to the Abbot and newspapers were rarely seen in the calefactory.

Boniface Natter was blessed as Abbot on 24th February 1903, by pure coincidence exactly 365 years after the closure of the medieval Abbey - 'the last day of a year of years', as Adam Hamilton put it. After the Blessing a cheque for £1000 was found in the collection plate from Dr. Macnamara, one of the Abbey's friends, and this money was used to complete the west wing of the monastery to provide much-needed cells, and rooms for the novitiate.[53] Abbot Natter also arranged for the medieval statue of Our Lady of Buckfast to be restored and installed in the temporary church. The lower part of this statue, now in the Lady Chapel, had been discovered in an old wall, still retaining some of its colouring and gilding;

---

[51] The evidence for the foundations belonging to the 12th century Cistercian monastery is discussed in the Devon Archaeological Society Proceedings No. 46, 1988: 'Excavations and Building Recording at Buckfast Abbey, Devon', by S. W. Brown, p. 65-7.

[52] The presence of a woman in the somewhat Spartan atmosphere of the enclosure was beneficial to the monks on one occasion: Lady Clifford was moved to pay for the installation of central heating!

[53] Amongst the first group of seven novices to occupy this new novitiate in 1904 were Br. John Stéphan, the Abbey's future historian and Br. Peter Schrode, the future master mason of the Abbey church.

Frederick Walters was given the task of restoring the upper part.[54]

A TRAGEDY

Abbot Natter was only 36 when he was elected, and his skills as a scholar and communicator - he was fluent in French, German, English and Italian - meant that he was asked to travel to give advice to other monasteries, with journeys to Mexico and the U.S.A. in 1904 and again to the U.S.A. in 1905. In 1906 he was chosen for the high office of Visitor to the French Province of the Subiaco Congregation and it was on his very first voyage as Visitor that, tragically, he was drowned.

The story of the shipwreck was told by Abbot Natter's fellow monk and travelling companion, Dom Anscar Vonier. Vonier had travelled on the Italian ship, the 'Sirio', from Genoa and it had been arranged that Abbot Natter would join the ship in Barcelona.

'It was the first day of our voyage to the Argentine, Saturday August 4th, 1906. I had not seen [Abbot Natter] for nearly twelve months as I had spent a year in Rome as a Professor at the College of S. Anselmo. I had a multitude of things whereon to question him about my brethren, from whom the call of duty had separated me.

'About three o'clock in the afternoon I left him on the upper deck and went below. I was about to return when suddenly there was a shock which, by the description of all who felt it, produced a most strange sensation; it was for me the impression that the deck of my cabin was being driven in.

'I went above in haste, through the midst of shattered mirrors and broken glass. On deck, I found the Abbot with two bishops and their companions. "What do you think about it?" I asked Father Abbot, as I joined him. "I think," he answered, "it is not dangerous if only all the people will remain quiet."

'At that moment the 'Sirio's siren screamed. "It would be wise," Father Abbot told me, "to go and fetch our lifebelts". These words were said with the utmost calmness, and with almost a smile on his lips. I went below, but could find only one belt; returning to the deck, I saw the bishops and priests on their knees, reciting the Act of Contrition. I put the lifebelt down by Father Abbot, who was also kneeling, and to this moment I cannot understand how he found himself without that means of safety when the vessel foundered. The fact remains that when he wished to put it on it had disappeared.

'But already we felt the deck shake beneath our feet. I knelt down and begged him to give me Absolution, and in his turn he knelt and received the same from

---

[54] Medieval Cistercian abbeys usually had St. Mary as their patron, and this dedication continued in the modern Buckfsat. The restored statue, therefore, has always been a potent symbol to the present community, symbolising both the physical and the spritiual link with its past.

me. *"Good-bye, Father Abbot; if we must die, we die content, we lose nothing," I said. "Good-bye, Father Anscar," he answered gravely, but with complete calm - not one word more. I drew myself away and hurried towards the bows, for we were on the stern deck, and the majority of the voyagers was further forward. I ran, therefore, to give them Absolution. But these unfortunates, by I know not what fatal instinct, rushed towards the stern, and I advanced into the midst of a dense and maddened crowd giving Absolution, several times finding my hand caught and passionately pressed.*

'Suddenly the stern deck was flooded with water with the rapidity of lightning, and the friends whom I had left, the crowds to whom I went, were all submerged. That was, in my opinion, the moment when the greater part of those who drowned were washed away.'[55]

The 'Sirio' did not in fact sink, but came to rest on the rocks it had struck. A French steamer and three Spanish fishing vessels came to the rescue and took about 550 people to the shore, which was still visible from the shipwreck. 382 people were reported missing. Anscar Vonier was looked after by a family in the coastal village of Cabo los Palos and returned to Buckfast three weeks later, to the great relief of the monks, who at one point had thought both Fr. Anscar and Abbot Boniface had drowned. Shortly after his arrival an election was held for a new Abbot, and Anscar Vonier was chosen. He was elected on September 14th 1906 and blessed on October 18th.

ABOVE: ANSCAR VONIER SOON AFTER HIS ELECTION AS ABBOT.
BELOW: THE FIRST LOAD OF STONES FOR THE CHURCH, 1906.

REBUILDING THE ABBEY CHURCH

Shortly after becoming Abbot, Anscar Vonier announced to the community that, having discussed the matter with Abbot Natter on board the 'Sirio', his first project would be to rebuild the Abbey church on its original foundations. As there was no building fund, the community itself would provide the builders, led by Br. Peter Schrode, who had been sent to the Abbey of En-Calcat in southern France in 1901, as an *alumnus*, to learn the art of masonry from the Benedictine master-masons working there.

'You will smile,' Abbot Anscar wrote to his friend , the Abbess of Dourgne, 'but you know very well that I am only thirty. In another thirty years time I shall not be so very old, and during all that time I shall apply myself to this task without ceasing. Given time and patience one might construct a world. I do not expect donations of large sums but shall look for small but regular contributions - and

---

[55] Quoted from 'Abbot of Buckfast - A Study of Anscar Vonier', Dom Ernest Graf, 1957, p. 35.

ABOVE: THE ABBEY CHURCH IN 1921.

BELOW: THE BUILDERS: BR. HILARION, BR. PETER, FR. RICHARD AND BR. IGNATIUS.

I shall know how to wait. Yesterday I spoke of my plan for the first time and on the spot I was handed one pound sterling. It is a beginning.'[56] In a letter of 15th December 1906 he wrote, 'In half an hour I expect the arrival of the first cartload of stone for our Abbey church', but it was not until January 5th 1907 that the whole community gathered at the north-east corner of the foundations and Abbot Anscar laid the first stone.

The Abbey church was built piecemeal, according to the funds that were available - but at no time did work come to a halt until the whole church was completed, thirty-two years later. The builders - normally only four monks, and never more than six[57] - began with the east end, the sanctuary, transepts and two bays of the nave, building onto the foundations, which had been restored up to ground level during the preceding years by the whole community during periods set aside for manual work. At first, while funds were low, all the stone had to be cut and dressed by the monks in temporary workshops erected to the north of the church, although in later years they were able to buy the stone ready-dressed from the quarries. Scaffolding was made from wooden poles, lashed together with ropes and chains. Stone was lifted with manual hoists or block and tackle.[58] The neighbouring farmer, John Beard, allowed the monks to take sand from his property; mixing quantities of sand and cement was one of the tasks undertaken by the whole community. The architect Frederick Walters had already designed the church but now sent more detailed plans for the actual construction. Thus the building work

proceeded, even through the First World War when the monks (two-thirds of whom were German) were prohibited from leaving the monastery without a special licence, besides having to endure the hostility of the local population.

Funds continued to come in: in 1910 Sir Robert Harvey, from Totnes, donated a superb peal of fourteen bells, in memory of his Peruvian wife, Alida. At first these were hung on the Abbot's Tower, before being installed in the church tower in 1920. At this time the tower had not been built to its final height, so there was no ringing chamber: the bells were rung from the balcony around the lantern tower. This was dangerous: on one occasion an inexperienced ringer was lifted from his feet and dangled over the lantern crossing! It was to accommodate such a fine set of bells that the tower was eventually raised to its present height.[59] Most of the furnishings in the church were also donated by individuals: the *champlevé* enamel Stations of the Cross, the carvings on the altars in the side-chapels, stained glass, candelabra, and the great Corona Lucis above the sanctuary, to name only a few.

ACCIDENTS

During the whole rebuilding project, there were only two accidents, in spite of the total lack of safety features, by modern standards of building practice. A collection of glass-plate photographs taken by one of the builders, Br. Ignatius, show the builders in flapping habits, with no helmets, no safety rails or guards on the scaffolding, working in what were effectively medieval conditions up to 150 feet above the ground. Some of these photos were used in a pack produced for schools to show the hazards of the construction industry!

The first accident took place during this early period of the rebuilding, and involved Br. Ignatius. He was working on the vaulting over the north transept and fell some 50 feet to the floor below. Miraculously, his fall was broken by some of the wooden scaffolding and he landed on a pile of sand: he did not even break any bones. At Compline every evening, some say he used to stand slightly apart from the community, on the exact spot where he fell, giving thanks to God for his preservation!

The second accident happened in the winter of 1931. Three of the monks (Br. Peter, Br. Paschal and a visiting Jordanian monk, Br. Placid) were coming down together on the stone barrow at the end of the day's work on the roof of the nave when the brakes of the hoist (by then an electric winch) failed and the three plunged to the ground. Br. Placid fractured his kneecap but Br. Peter and Br. Paschal, although shocked, were not hurt.

After the Inauguration of the church by Cardinal Bourne on August 3rd, 1922, when the church was opened for

---

[56] Dom Ernest Graf, *ibid*, p. 46.

[57] The original builders were Br. Peter (master mason), Fr. Richard, Br. Hilarion and Br. Ignatius. Br. Paschal joined the community in 1927 and took over from Br. Ignatius. A Dutch monk, Br. Gabriel Mokveld, learnt his trade at Buckfast in 1921 (as Br. Peter had done in France in 1901) before building the Abbey of Mt. St. Benedict in Trinidad and many other churches and schools in the West Indies. Br. Placid Sa'ad, a Jordanian from the Priory of Ss. Benedict and Ephrem in Jerusalem, joined the builders from 1931-1933. The builders were responsible for masonry work; specialists were engaged for much of the decoration.

[58] Br. Ignatius designed and built an electric hoist in 1912; he was also responsible for wiring the whole church. The Abbey was the first home in the area to install domestic electricity, in 1902, using the water-powered turbines in the Spinning Mill when the factory was closed at night. This was done by Fr. Denys Matthieu, who also later installed street lighting in Buckfastleigh at the request of the Town Council, but the system soon broke down.

[59] A fifteenth bell, the magnificent bourdon bell named 'Hosanna', ringing a full octave lower than the lowest tenor bell of the original set, was donated in 1935 by Miss Hilda de Trafford.

worship, the builders were given a few months' rest before continuing with the second stage of the project: the nave and west front. The latter was entirely donated by Henry and Josephine Schiller, and included the porch, gallery, chapel, baptistery and the great bronze font; they even paid for the stone to be dressed at the quarry, saving the monks some three years' work. The Schillers also donated the golden High Altar and two hundred acres of farmland.

EARNING A LIVING

Meanwhile, the Abbey had to develop other sources of income, as the donations were all related to the rebuilding of the church. In medieval times most abbeys had survived off the rents and tithes from their endowments, but not so in modern times: Buckfast Abbey had to be self-supporting. For their own needs, the monks grew vegetables all around the Abbey and kept bees, pigs and dairy cattle, but there were many expenses so a financial income was also required. Several ideas were tried out over the years - some successful, some not. Undoubtedly the greatest success was 'Buckfast Tonic Wine', which had venerable precedents in the wines and spirits traditionally produced in monasteries throughout Europe. The recipe for the wine had been sent to Buckfast in 1897 by the nephew of Dom Denys Matthieu, one of the original French monks. It used a fortified base wine from Spain to which macerated maté tea, coca leaves and vanilla had been added. It was sold at the Abbey as a medicinal wine with the directions on the label: 'Three small glasses per day'. By the 1920s 1400 bottles were sold annually, 500 of them at Buckfast and the others by post, but in 1927 the local magistrates withdrew the Abbey's licence to sell

MAKING TONIC WINE, 1932.

the wine. Consequently the sole agency was given to a London wine merchant who was able to develop the business with the Abbey receiving a percentage from the sales, which increased dramatically through energetic advertising campaigns.[60] The base wine continued to come in bulk to Buckfast where the recipe was applied, before being sent to London where the wine merchant - J. Chandler and Company - bottled and distributed it far and wide. Buckfast Tonic Wine has continued to be a source of income for the Abbey until the present day.

THE ABBEY BEGINS TO ATTRACT TOURISTS

It was during the 1920s and 1930s that the Abbey began to attract visitors. As early as 1907 the gateway into the grounds, by the North Gate, had been widened so as to make it easier for people to see the building work proceeding. Although major donors provided most of the funds at first, it was through the donations of the increasing numbers of

---

[60] Particularly notable were the advertising campaigns in cinema foyers in the 1930s. Outside Errol Flynn's 'Robin Hood', for example, could be seen a display of Tonic Wine and the slogan, 'All the Poor Men Blessed Robin Hood - Buckfast Does the Whole World Good'. In another campaign the slogan was, 'Of Paramount importance see "The Barrier" and raise the barrier to health with Buckfast Tonic Wine'. In Dublin, the wine was advertised on 4,500,000 tram tickets. In Hong Kong it was marketed as 'The dew on the grass in the early morning'!

visitors that work continued day by day in the latter stages of the rebuilding. As road travel improved, more and more people visited, causing concern - even outrage - amongst some local people. 'From morning until late evening,' wrote a Buckfast villager to the 'Western Morning News' in 1928, 'the inhabitants of Buckfast, Protestant and Catholic alike, find themselves and their children in danger every moment from the never ending train of motor cars and charabancs.' Visitors continued to come in ever-increasing numbers, however, and the monks opened tea rooms in the cottage by the North Gate, re-establishing a tradition of hospitality for visitors which had disappeared from Buckfast in 1539 when the Guest Hall was demolished.

THE CONSECRATION

25th August 1932 was the day chosen for the Consecration of the Abbey Church: after 25 years of labour all but the upper section of the tower had been completed. Cardinal Bourne was chosen by the Pope as his representative; also taking part were five Archbishops, sixteen Bishops, thirty Abbots and many priests and members of religious orders. Not only was the church full to capacity, but thousands heard the ceremony outside, where loudspeakers had been installed. The Cardinal's sermon was broadcast by the B.B.C., and the whole consecration made the front pages of the national press. In his address, Abbot Anscar said, 'All that you see here is truly the fruit of faith. We have had no other talent or genius except the talent or genius of faith.'

The final phase of the rebuilding of the church was the completion of the tower to accommodate the superb set of bells which had been donated in 1910. Because of the great height of the scaffolding required for this, the builders designed a special fitting to secure the chains at the joints. Br. Paschal described the sensation of standing on this scaffolding on a windy day, when it was the *tower*, not the scaffolding which appeared to be swaying! The worst moment, he said, was when they had to fix the winch on a pole above the highest pinnacle, before lifting the final capping stone into position! This final stone was laid on the tower on 24th July 1937, completing thirty two years work, but it was not until December of the following year that the pointing was finished and the scaffolding removed.

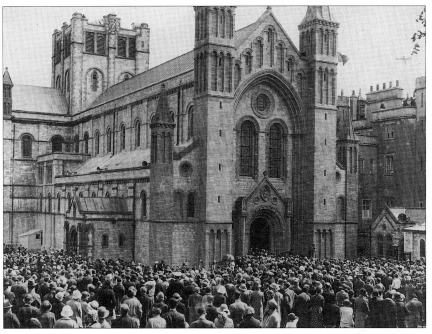

CROWDS AT THE CONSECRATION OF THE ABBEY CHURCH, 25TH AUGUST 1932.

ABBOT VONIER'S LIFE'S WORK COMPLETE

Abbot Anscar was away from Buckfast on a lecture tour in the last weeks of 1938, returning on December 6th. The builders had hurried to remove the scaffolding for his return, so that Vonier, exhausted and ill with a cold he had caught during the long journey home, could see the great work completed. Three weeks later he was dead.

Tributes to Anscar Vonier flowed in. He was known internationally as a writer, preacher and scholar - indeed his fame endures in Europe primarily as a theologian - but of course it was his life's work as a builder for which he was most famous in Britain. A letter in the 'Daily Telegraph' described a particularly apposite conversation the writer had recently had with the Abbot: 'Once the church is completed and the whole building finished,' Abbot Anscar had said, 'I have done my task and I can go.' The monks applied to the Home Office for permission to bury him in the sanctuary of the church and were told that permission was not required as it had been used for burial before - in the Middle Ages. A bronze memorial plaque, showing the achievements of Anscar Vonier's life, was made by Benno Elkan, an Austrian Jew who had been sheltered at Buckfast by the (German) Abbot during Hitler's persecutions.

ABOVE: FITTING THE FINAL STONE ONTO THE CHURCH TOWER, 24TH JULY 1937.
BELOW: ABBOT BRUNO FEHRENBACHER.

ABBOT BRUNO FEHRENBACHER

The community was at still predominantly German, and it was another German who was chosen as Abbot Anscar's successor: Bruno Fehrenbacher. During the 1930s the community had grown, with almost all of the new members British-born, making Buckfast truly international. In Europe as a whole, meanwhile, international relations were fast deteriorating and shortly after his election Abbot Bruno had to face the ordeal of guiding his community through

another World War. Five of the English monks became Army Chaplains and one French lay-brother was mobilised by his government. The older, German members remained at Buckfast, where the Abbey took part in the British war effort, manning the local firefighters' force, farming intensively and offering a refuge for the staff and 100 pupils of St. Boniface College, Plymouth.

Although the building had been completed, there was still work to be done in the church. Here the influence of one of the younger British monks, Dom Charles Norris, began to be felt. He began to make stained glass at Buckfast in 1932, as well as producing works of art in other media. Having trained at the Royal College of Art in mural painting, he painted the Lantern Tower ceiling in egg-tempera in 1939; one of his helpers remembers hearing the news of the outbreak of war while finishing some of the gold-leaf work. Dom Charles also learned the art of mosaic flooring at this time. The marble pavements in the Sanctuary and Crossing were made in 1943 and 1947,[61] and Fr. Charles designed the pavement in the Choir in 1948 and laid the Lady Chapel floor in 1958. Fr. Charles's greatest impact on the church, however, was through

---

[61] These mosaic floors were made by the London-based specialists, Fennings, under the artistic direction of Marcus Reader and the supervision of Edmund Buckley. The floors used the *Opus Alexandrinum* technique, where pieces of fine coloured marble complement each other in simple geometric shapes.

his modern stained glass, done in the *dalles-de-verre* technique in which thick 'tiles of glass' are chipped to shape and laid mosaic-fashion in a matrix of resin. His masterpiece is the huge east window in the Blessed Sacrament Chapel (1968), showing Christ at the Last Supper. Here, he achieves a fusion between medieval and modern styles, emphasising the qualities of the material - thick slabs of luminous pot-melted glass which bathe the chapel with coloured light - while fitting it into a modern context, and on a scale only made possible by modern materials and building techniques. After the Second War, when Plymouth was being rebuilt, Buckfast supplied windows for many new churches, as well as many other modern churches further afield.

IN SEARCH OF THE BEST STRAINS OF BEES

Another monk who came to the fore during the abbacy of Bruno Fehrenbacher was Br. Adam Kehrle. He had become head beekeeper at Buckfast in 1919, just after the Isle of Wight disease (*acarine*) had wiped out 30 of the Abbey's 46 hives. Br. Adam made it his life's work to breed a new strain of bee which would withstand disease whilst also being hardy, quiet, slow to swarm and a good honey producer. He set up a breeding station in the middle of Dartmoor, isolated from roving drones from other hives, and began the painstaking work of cross-breeding. In 1950 he asked Abbot Bruno and the community to back his plan to travel throughout Europe in search of pure strains of indigenous bees to provide stock for his breeding programme. With support from the Ministry of Agriculture, Adam was bought an Austin A40 (at that time only doctors and midwives were eligible for new cars) and on March 20th 1950 he set out on his own, aiming deliberately for the most isolated rural areas where the original indigenous strains would not have been cross-bred. Many more such journeys followed and over the next forty years he travelled more than 100,000 miles through Western Europe, Asia Minor and North Africa, sweet-talking beekeepers to part with a few queens which he could send back to England by post - some to Buckfast and some to the Ministry's of Agriculture's Bee Research Department at Harpenden. The result of his breeding programme was a new strain - the 'Buckfast Bee'. Br. Adam became known throughout the world for his research and was awarded the O.B.E. in 1974. He remained head beekeeper until 1992, when he retired at the age of 93.[62]

BROTHER ADAM KEHRLE

CONTROVERSY AT FOUNTAINS

Buckfast had gained a national reputation for its revival on a medieval site, and in 1946 the Abbey became briefly involved in a more controversial restoration project. A group of Roman Catholics planned to buy Fountains Abbey, with the intention of inviting monks from Buckfast to restore it and re-found it as a Benedictine monastery and as a memorial for Catholics who had died in the two world wars. A national outcry followed: Fountains Abbey was obviously

[62] Br. Adam's biography is 'For the Love of Bees' by Lesley Bill, 1989. His own books include 'Beekeeping at Buckfast Abbey' (1975) and 'In Search of the Best Strains of Bees' (1983).

nearer to the heart of the nation as a romantic ruin than as a working monastery. Br. Peter visited the site and expressed his own reluctance: so much of the abbey was still standing that the practical difficulties of making good the crumbling medieval walls would be a much harder task than he had faced at Buckfast. The plan was soon abandoned and the ruins were eventually sold to the National Trust.

In the summer of 1956 Abbot Bruno's health deteriorated and, on medical advice, he decided to resign, taking instead the less onerous post of assistant chaplain to the Benedictine nuns of Stanbrook, near Worcester. Until the election of a new Abbot, the novice-master, Dom Placid Hooper, acted as Superior.

ABBOT PLACID HOOPER

At the election in January 1957, Dom Placid was chosen as the next Abbot. He became the first English Abbot of Buckfast since the Reformation, reflecting what was now a predominantly British community. One of his first actions was to begin the process of changing Buckfast's affiliation from the Subiaco Congregation to the English Benedictine Congregation. This had been planned for many years and was finally approved by the Abbot President in 1960. Several changes came about as a result. The E.B.C. abbeys were a close-knit family, so Buckfast took on a number of 'cousins', and links developed between them. The changeover introduced various differences in the monastic day and there was a minor alteration to the habit. Abbots would now be elected for an eight-year term of office rather than for life. But by far the greatest change was the adoption of the English Benedictine tradition in education. Many of the other monasteries in the E.B.C. had schools - Downside, Ampleforth and Douai are among

ABOVE: ABBOT PLACID HOOPER BELOW: ABBOT LEO SMITH.

the best known - and Buckfast opened its own boys' preparatory school in 1967. This involved the preparation of a teaching staff from the community, several of whom were sent to Oxford, Cambridge and London to train as teachers, and another substantial building project. The school was built to the north of the church, and opened in September 1967 with Dom Cuthbert Smith as the first headmaster. It thrived for 27 years until changes in educational trends (such as a move away from boarding) forced it to close in 1994.

Other changes took place during Placid Hooper's abbacy as a result of the Second Vatican Council (1963) - a radical re-think of the whole Roman Catholic Church which had a considerable effect on monastic life as well. Most of the changes concerned the Liturgy: priests were no longer required to say Mass individually but could all celebrate together, now facing the congregation; also, although some Latin was still used, more English came into the services. On a more social level, the lay-brothers, who had been the Abbey's 'working class', living in separate lodgings, without a vote in Chapter, were now given equal status to the choir monks.

ABBOT LEO SMITH

Abbot Placid served for two terms of office, until 1976, when the community elected Dom Leo Smith as the fifth Abbot since the restoration. By the late 1970s Buckfast Abbey was amongst the most-visited places in the West

Country, attracting some 300,000 holidaymakers each year, but the facilities for these visitors were inadequate, with the result that some of the fears expressed by villagers in the 1920s (see page 31) had become a reality: queues of cars and coaches filled the roads and a plethora of small tourist businesses had grown up near the Abbey.

As a result, during Abbot Leo's two terms of office, perhaps the main feature was the start of a major redevelopment of the precinct - certainly the greatest building programme since the completion of the church, and a recognition by the monks that their ministry included visitors whose time at the Abbey was very brief, as well as parishioners. The overseeing architect for all these developments was Richard Riley. A new car park was made (1982) followed by a gift shop (1983) and restaurant (1991). Each new development was preceded by archaeological excavation, adding further to our knowledge of the medieval Abbey - and indeed influencing the design of the new buildings themselves so that they fitted in well with the other stone and slate medieval buildings around the precinct. Meanwhile, so that the visitors could pick up something of the ethos of the Abbey during their short stay, an exhibition was set up in the crypt under the Chapel of the Blessed Sacrament (1982), as well as an Audio/Visual show (1985). An education service was established in 1985 to develop facilities for schools wishing to visit the Abbey and find out more about its life. An ever-increasing lay staff was taken on to manage most of these facilities for the visitors, including a commercial director and an accountant. By 1990 the number of lay-staff was similar to the number of monks - about 45.

ABBOT DAVID CHARLESWORTH

Abbot David Charlesworth was elected in 1992 while Abbot Leo took over as head beekeeper from Br. Adam, with whom he had travelled on some of his European journeys in search of new strains of bees. Two significant developments were completed during Abbot David's first year of office. The first was the restoration of the late medieval south wing of the Guest Hall using oak from the Abbey's own woodlands. The second development was the conversion of the medieval South Gate into a residential centre for retreats, and for the Abbey's guests - another example of continuity, as the building had first been built as an almshouse and was now returning to a similar use. The number of visitors also led to the reorganisation of the Abbey precinct in order to preserve quieter areas for the community.

ABBOT DAVID CHARLESWORTH

MEDIEVAL INTO MODERN

In the century since monks returned to Buckfast, we have seen history repeat itself so many times: building works which echo their medieval predecessors, not from any conscious desire to recreate the past but because they were to be put to the same use; activities - such as beekeeping, winemaking or welcoming visitors - which came about because of the same circumstances that had existed five centuries earlier; above all, a routine of prayer and worship almost identical to that of the medieval abbey, and a Rule with guidelines for community living which are as relevant today as they were in 1018. It is not History that is important in the story of Buckfast but Continuity, and Faith.

ABBOTS OF BUCKFAST

known from historical sources.

Benedictine:

Alwin (Aelwinus)   first mentioned as having attended a Shire-mote in Exeter in about 1040. Known from the Domesday Book to have been Abbot in 1066.

Savignac:

Eustace   first mentioned in 1143 in a Totnes Deed. He was Abbot when Buckfast was affiliated to the Abbey of Citeaux (Cistercian) in 1147.

Cistercian:

William   acted as Papal Legate in 1190.
Nicholas   elected in 1205.
Michael   mentioned in the Cartulary of Buckfast Abbey (C.B.A.) in 1223.
Peter   mentioned in the C.B.A. 1242.
William (II)   mentioned in the C.B.A. 1249.
Howell   mentioned in the Leger Book (L.B.) of Buckfast (Brit. Mus.) - no dates.
Henry   mentioned in C.B.A. 1264 and 1269.
Simon   mentioned in C.B.A. and Petre Archives (P.A.) between 1273 and 1280.
Robert   mentioned in L.B. and Exeter Episcopal Registers (Ep. Reg.) between 1280 and 1283.
Peter de Colepitte   mentioned in the P.A. between 1291 and 1313
Robert (II)   mentioned in the Ep. Reg. 1316.
William Atte Slade   mentioned in the Banco Rolls 1327.
Stephen   mentioned in the Ep. Reg. 1328.
John of Churchstowe   mentioned in the Ep. Reg. 1332.
William Gifford   mentioned in the Ep. Reg. 1333.
Stephen of Cornwall   mentioned in the Ep. Reg. 1348.
Philip (Beaumont)   mentioned in the Ep. Reg. 1349.
Robert Symons   mentioned in the Ep. Reg. and P.A. between 1355 and 1390.
William Paderstow   mentioned in the Ep. Reg and P.A. 1395.
William Slade   mentioned in the Ep. Reg. and by Leland - "Com. de Scriptoribus Britanniae" and Boase - "Annals of Exeter College, Oxford" between 1401 and 1415.
William Beaghe   mentioned in the Ep. Reg. and P.A. between 1415 and 1432.
Thomas Roger   mentioned in Ep. Reg. and P.A. Blessed as Abbot in 1432. Had been Prior Administrator for about 10 years before this.
John Ffytchett   mentioned in the Ep. Reg. 1440.
John Matthu (Matthew)   mentioned in the Ep. Reg. 1449.
John King   mentioned in the Statutes of the General Chapter of the Cistercian Order from 1464 to 1498.
John Rede   mentioned in the Ep. Reg. 1498.
John Bleworthy   mentioned in 1505 - Cal. of Early Chancery Proceedings, also in Powderham MSS.
Alfred Gyll   mentioned in the Ep. Reg. 1512.
John Rede (II)   mentioned in the Ep. Reg. 1525.
Gabriel Donne   imposed on the community in 1535 by Thomas Cromwell (State papers). He surrendered the Abbey to the King on 25th February, 1539.

Monastic Life was restored at Buckfast in 1882.

Benedictine:

Boniface Natter   elected 19th November, 1902. Died 4th August, 1906.
Anscar Vonier   elected 14th September, 1906. Died 26th December, 1938.
Bruno Fehrenbacher   elected 10th January, 1939. Resigned 1956. Titular Abbot of Tavistock until his death on 18th July, 1965.
Placid Hooper   elected 5th January 1957. Ruling Abbot till 1976. Titular Abbot of Tavistock until his death on 11th December, 1995.
Leo Smith   elected 30th January, 1976. Ruling Abbot till 1992. Titular Abbot of Colchester.
David Charlesworth   elected 3rd January, 1992.